GAYLORD

FROZEN MAN

▾ D A V I D G E T Z ▾

FROZEN MAN

Illustrated by
Peter McCarty

A Redfeather Book

HENRY HOLT AND COMPANY/NEW YORK

Acknowledgments

Thanks to the following people for the time
in personal interviews they gave me:
John Alexander, Christopher Bergman,
Markus Egg, David Fryer, John Gurche,
Janet Levy, and Konrad Spindler.

Henry Holt and Company, Inc.
Publishers since 1866
115 West 18th Street
New York, New York 10011

Henry Holt is a registered
trademark of Henry Holt and Company, Inc.

Published in Canada by Fitzhenry & Whiteside Ltd.,
195 Allstate Parkway, Markham, Ontario L3R 4T8.

Library of Congress Cataloging-in-Publication Data
Getz, David.
Frozen man / David Getz; illustrated by Peter McCarty.
p.   cm.—(A Redfeather book)
Includes bibliographical references.
1. Copper age—Italy—Trentino-Alto Adige—Juvenile literature.
2. Mummies—Italy—Trentino-Alto Adige—Juvenile literature.
3. Trentino-Alto Adige (Italy)—Antiquities—Juvenile literature.
I. Title.   II. Series: Redfeather books.
GN776.22.I8G47   1994   937'.3—dc20   94-9109

ISBN 0-8050-3261-4

First Edition—1994

Printed in the United States of America
on acid-free paper. ∞

1   3   5   7   9   10   8   6   4   2

For Jacqui, who has held my hand
across many mountains,
and Maxine, who will skip
from peak to peak.

▾   ▾   ▾

Thanks, of course, to my father—
this is your book, Dad—
and to Mom, and Karen.
And "Grandma Gabby."
And to Laura.

CONTENTS

FROZEN MAN

N obody knew what stories the body could tell.

On September 19, 1991, German tourists Erika and Helmut Simon had just climbed Finail Peak, the second-highest summit in the Ötztal Alps. Deciding to try something new, they took an unmarked path back down across the Similaun Glacier to their lodge. They spotted the body at an altitude of about 10,500 feet, nearly two miles above sea level. It lay near the border of Italy and Austria.

At first glance they thought they had come upon an abandoned doll. Getting closer, they both realized that the body was an adult man. Still frozen to the glacier, the dead man seemed to have risen from the ice, as if he was getting out of a pool. He appeared to be naked. His face was pressed down into the snow.

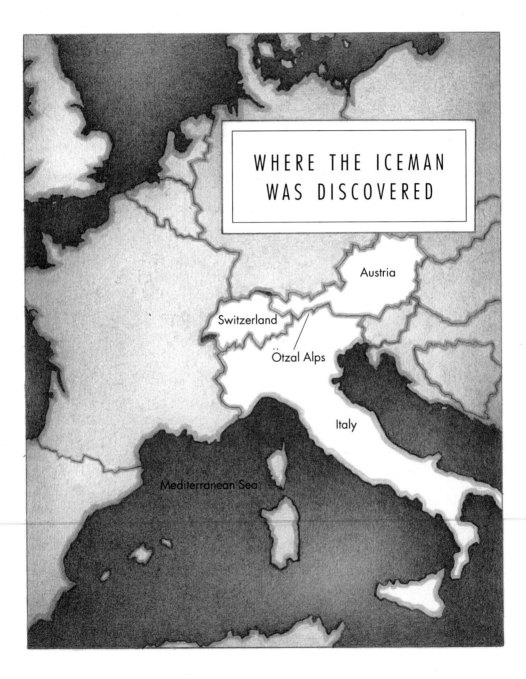

WHERE THE ICEMAN
WAS DISCOVERED

Austria

Switzerland

Ötzal Alps

Italy

Mediterranean Sea

The Simons discovered a small hole in the back of the victim's head. Suspicious that the man had been murdered, they rushed to a hikers' shelter to report the crime.

Markus Pirpomer, the owner of the shelter, called both the Italian and the Austrian police. The Italian authorities showed no interest. They assumed the body was simply another victim of a mountaineering accident. The Austrian authorities agreed to send over an officer. That summer they had already retrieved the bodies of eight accident victims from the snow and ice of the Alps.

When Markus Pirpomer reached the body, it struck him as remarkably different from other bodies that had emerged from the glacier.

A glacier is a river of ice. As snow on mountains gets deeper and heavier, it gradually turns into ice that can be hundreds of feet thick. Sometimes glaciers flow slowly down mountains.

Pirpomer knew that it wasn't unusual for a hiker to die in the Alps, get covered by falling snow, and be trapped in a glacier. He knew that as a glacier moves down a mountain, it occasionally reveals a body it captured higher up. These bodies are usually horribly crushed and mangled from being dragged by the massive glacier over rocks and boulders.

Pirpomer noticed that the body the Simons had discovered was remarkably intact. It was in the position of someone who had stretched out to take a nap. How could a man dragged down a mountain under tons of ice appear nearly undamaged?

Just as puzzling to Pirpomer was the body's skin. Being trapped in a glacier prevents oxygen from reaching a body's soft tissues. This turns the skin, muscles, and fat into adipocere, or "grave wax," a creamy or waxy substance that makes these victims appear to be made of soap or plaster.

This man was brown and leathery, as dried out as an Egyptian mummy. How could this happen to a man surrounded by ice and snow? Pirpomer suspected that there was something remarkable about this victim. He guessed that this man had died a long time ago, though how long ago he couldn't be sure.

The Austrian policeman arrived the afternoon of September 20. He had no reason to believe there was anything special about the body. He had no idea that this "Iceman" had come from a place no one alive had ever seen. He had no idea that the Iceman had brought with him strange tools and clothing from that distant place. They were buried along with him in the ice. The Iceman's body and his clothing and tools were like the pieces of a puzzle, waiting to be put back together.

The policeman nearly destroyed everything. He brought a jackhammer to free the body. He drilled right through the Iceman's hip, shattering the bone. He also ripped to shreds what turned out to be remains of the Iceman's cloak. By luck, the jackhammer ran out of power before it could do further harm. The officer contacted his superiors. He made plans to resume his efforts the following week. It was the next time a helicopter would be available to return him to the site.

Before he left, the policeman took some photographs. He also discovered a crude hand ax. It consisted of a small, tongue-shaped blade stuck into the end of an L-shaped branch. The policeman removed the ax as possible evidence of a crime.

Word began to spread about the man in ice. The next day, six mountaineers visited the body. They tried to free it but failed. Before leaving, they also took some photographs.

On September 22, the chairman of the Austrian mountain rescue team arrived with a friend. Together they freed the body, using a pickax, then informed the local police it was ready to be retrieved. The two also

Mountaineers visit the ancient body, still frozen in ice. *Copyright Paul Hanny / Gamma Liaison*

carried away from the site the remains of the Iceman's clothing, along with what was probably his backpack frame, part of a bow, and some clumps of grass. They left these objects at a local hotel in the Ötz valley.

The following day Rainer Henn found a note on his desk, informing him of this man in ice. Henn, the director of forensic medicine (medicine related to crimes and accidents) at the University of Innsbruck, had already examined six bodies that had emerged from glaciers that year. One of those victims had died in 1934, 57 years ago. Transformed by adipocere and terribly mutilated, the victim had resembled a damaged statue. Henn had found railway tickets and a membership card to a mountaineering club in the victim's pockets. But Henn had heard nothing of the condition of this body, the strange ax, or any of the other objects found at the site. Who would this new victim turn out to be?

Each year the Alps prove too treacherous for some skiers or hikers. The weather can change suddenly. Warm sunshine can instantly become a blinding snowstorm. At the altitude, or height, where the body was found, the air is thin. Breathing is difficult. It's easy to become tired and careless, to stumble and fall. Each year about 200 people lose their lives in the Alps from accidents or exposure to the cold.

When Henn arrived by helicopter at the site, he was surprised to discover another helicopter already there. It belonged to an Austrian television crew. The man in ice was making the news. There were rumors that he might be over 500 years old.

Though freed from the ice the previous day, the body had refrozen into the surrounding slush overnight. Not having brought any tools along with him, Henn was forced to borrow an ice pick and some ski poles to chip the body free. Like Pirpomer, Henn was immediately struck by the condition of the body. He wondered why it hadn't developed adipocere. He guessed that somehow the body had completely dried out, or mummified, before it was captured within the glacier. Then he discovered a dagger. It was made with a wooden handle and had a small stone blade.

What was this twentieth-century hiking victim doing with a tool from the Stone Age?

Henn immediately ordered his helpers to proceed with caution. This body is old, he told them.

With great effort Henn and his helpers removed the body from the ice, wrapped it in plastic, and forced it into a wooden coffin. It was then transported by helicopter and ambulance to the nearest morgue. The objects that had been found alongside the body were gath-

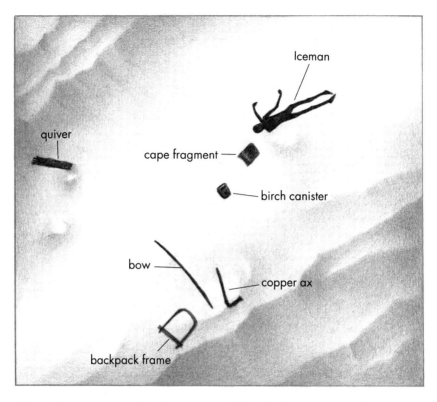

The placement of the Iceman and his belongings as they were found in the gap between two large rock formations.

ered and sent along. Henn's next step, by Austrian law, would be to perform an autopsy on the body to determine its cause of death.

The Iceman was about to be cut open and taken apart like a laboratory frog.

Fortunately archaeologist Konrad Spindler got to the

body first. As dean of the Institute for Pre- and Protohistory at the University of Innsbruck, Konrad Spindler is an expert on life in the Alps. Having heard some of the rumors about the man in ice, Spindler contacted Henn and expressed an interest in seeing the body and the objects found alongside it.

Spindler got his wish the following morning. He was astonished. The objects appeared to be the tools someone would carry if he was wandering around the mountains thousands of years ago! And then there was the body. Though his hip was damaged, the Iceman had arrived from the distant past remarkably whole. Scientists would be able to study his body as well as any doctor studying a patient.

Though brown, leathery, dried out, and somewhat hideous to look at, the Iceman was probably the most magnificent sight Konrad Spindler had ever witnessed.

"I felt like Howard Carter when he opened the coffin of Tutankhamen—King Tut—and saw the golden face of the pharaoh," Spindler said. "From that first moment I saw that we would want to spend a lot of time studying this man and his equipment. This is one of the most remarkable archaeological discoveries of the century."

Helmut and Erika Simon had discovered a prehistoric man, possibly on his way to work. Who was this man? How did he live? How did he die? When did he last walk the paths of the Alps, and what could he tell us about his world? As chief archaeologist at the University of Innsbruck, Spindler would head the team of scientists that would seek to answer those questions.

The first step was to get the Iceman to reveal his secrets. How could scientists learn when he lived?

What clues did the Iceman offer? Simply looking at his body, scientists couldn't tell if he died 2,000 or 8,000 years ago. True, he was brown and leathery and so dried out that he weighed 29 pounds. The dehydration must have taken some time. And the shape of his face had been changed by the weight of the ice continuously pressing down on him. This too must have taken a long time. But how long?

Spindler turned to the Iceman's artifacts for clues. Artifacts are any objects that are made by people. To learn about ancient people, archaeologists study what artifacts are made of, how they are made, and what they were used for. The Iceman's artifacts were particularly

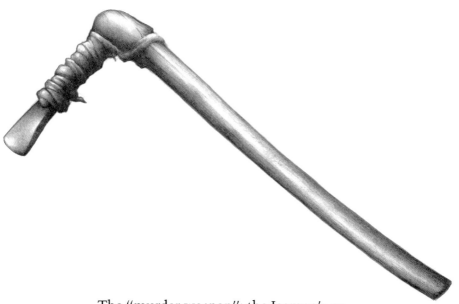

The "murder weapon": the Iceman's ax

fascinating. What was the man in ice doing with a dagger with a stone blade? Why didn't he have a Swiss Army knife with a stainless-steel blade? Daggers with stone blades hadn't been used in Europe for thousands of years!

Then there was that "murder weapon," the ax. Its shaft was made from an L-shaped branch of a yew tree. Like the dagger blade, that shaft also belonged to a period in Europe called the Stone Age. The Stone Age began in Europe about a million years ago and ended about 5,000 years ago. During this period people used stones, such as flint, for their tools. The Iceman had been found with a stone knife blade and two arrows with stone points. Could he have lived during the Stone Age?

No, he couldn't, was Spindler's first guess. The Iceman's ax appeared to be bronze. Stone Age people didn't have the technology to make bronze tools.

The Bronze Age followed the Stone Age. It began in Europe about 5,000 years ago and lasted for nearly 2,000 years. During this time people in Europe began to master the technique of melting copper in furnaces that reached 1,981 degrees Fahrenheit and alloying it with tin to make bronze.

If the ax's blade was bronze, its Stone-Age-style handle suggested it was made at the beginning of the Bronze Age.

"The archaeological dating can't be wrong," Spindler said. "So the ax dates from approximately 2,000 B.C., or 2,000 years before the birth of Christ."

If the policeman's suspicions were correct, then the ax would be evidence of a crime committed over 4,000 years ago.

The next step was to test Spindler's hypothesis scientifically. The archaeologists working with Spindler returned to the Iceman's body. They removed tiny fragments of the hipbone damaged by the policeman. About an ounce, or the weight of a paper clip, was sent to Robert Hedges at his Oxford University laboratory in England. Hedges would count how many atoms of carbon 14 the bone still contained. This would help him tell when the Iceman died.

All living things take in carbon. Plants absorb it as they "breathe" in carbon dioxide. People absorb it by eating plants or by eating animals that eat plants. A small but constant percentage of that carbon is carbon 14, which is radioactive. It is continually decaying, or coming apart.

If we look at the carbon atoms as marbles, then a sample of something that was once alive, such as a piece of bone, can be compared to a jar filled with trillions of marbles. In that jar are just a handful of strange marbles. While all the other marbles remain the same over thousands of years, the strange ones, the carbon-14 marbles, slowly disappear.

When a person dies, he or she stops taking in carbon. The quantity of regular carbon (carbon 12) stays the same, but the quantity of carbon 14 gets smaller and smaller as the carbon 14 atoms decay. The rate of this decay is as precise as the ticking of a clock. A slow clock! It takes 5,730 years for half the carbon 14 in a sample to tick away and disappear.

After counting the carbon 14 in the sample of bone, Hedges determined that the Iceman died about 5,300 years ago. This placed him more than 1,000 years farther back in time than Spindler's estimate. Hedges's carbon-14 dating pushed the Iceman backward out of the Bronze Age into the end of the Stone Age.

Scientists in Zurich, Switzerland, used another sample of the Iceman for radiocarbon dating. They followed the same procedures as Hedges. They arrived at a similar answer. The Iceman was clearly over 5,000 years old.

But what about that ax? How could a man who lived during the Stone Age carry a bronze tool that wasn't invented for another thousand years or so? That was like finding a computer buried beside a Viking.

Dietrich Ankner, a metallurgist at the Roman-Germanic Museum in Mainz, Germany, analyzed the ax blade. Bronze is an alloy of copper and tin. If Ankner found any tin in the composition of the blade, that would indicate it was bronze. His tests showed no tin. This meant the blade was almost pure copper.

Spindler had made a reasonable mistake. Copper and bronze look the same to the naked eye.

The Iceman lived more than 3,000 years before the invention of gunpowder or paper. Carbon-14 dating placed him in Europe over 3,000 years before Julius Caesar ruled the Roman Empire, 2,000 years before the first Olympic Games in Greece, and more than 700 years before Imhotep designed the first pyramid in Egypt. He roamed the Alps at a time when the wheel was a new invention! His contemporaries in central Europe lived in wooden houses that were built on stilts above the shorelines of lakes. These villages were often surrounded by a fence. Inside, people raised wheat and barley, kept animals in pens, and probably considered cooked dog a pretty good meal. Cheese was also a new invention. They used deer antler and chipped stone for tools. They buried their dead in rows in huge stone tombs. Men were placed on their right side, females on their left side. People were buried with what they would need in the afterlife: axes, knives, and beads.

Since the Iceman died on his way to work, he wasn't buried in a tomb. Even so, the Iceman is the oldest, best-preserved body ever discovered.

A number of chance events made the Iceman's trip to the present possible.

Most creatures disappear shortly after they die, espe-

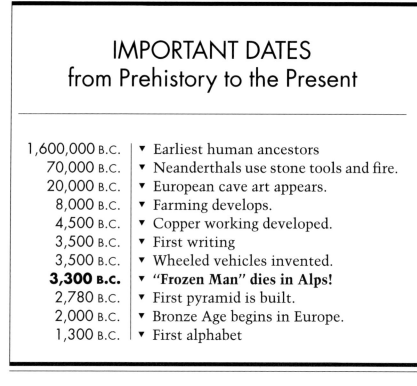

IMPORTANT DATES
from Prehistory to the Present

1,600,000 B.C.	▾ Earliest human ancestors
70,000 B.C.	▾ Neanderthals use stone tools and fire.
20,000 B.C.	▾ European cave art appears.
8,000 B.C.	▾ Farming develops.
4,500 B.C.	▾ Copper working developed.
3,500 B.C.	▾ First writing
3,500 B.C.	▾ Wheeled vehicles invented.
3,300 B.C.	▾ **"Frozen Man" dies in Alps!**
2,780 B.C.	▾ First pyramid is built.
2,000 B.C.	▾ Bronze Age begins in Europe.
1,300 B.C.	▾ First alphabet

cially if they die and are left out in the open, as the Iceman was. Blood stops flowing in their veins, and the body starts to decay. Scavengers, such as vultures, rodents, and insects, dine on the decaying body. Flies lay

Most B.C. ("before Christ") dates are approximate. Add 2,000 years to every B.C. date to see how many years ago the event took place. Dates are taken from the *New York Public Library Desk Reference.*

776 B.C.	▼ First Olympic Games are held in Greece.
753 B.C.	▼ Rome is founded.
221 B.C.	▼ Invention of gunpowder
215 B.C.	▼ Great Wall of China is built.
76 B.C.	▼ Julius Caesar begins his reign over Roman Empire.
5 B.C.	▼ Jesus Christ is born.

932	▼ Printed books are developed in China.
1000	▼ Papermaking invented
1000	▼ Vikings begin exploration of North America
1360	▼ Mechanical clock is invented.
1492	▼ Columbus discovers West Indies
1911	▼ X Rays discovered
1947	▼ Radiocarbon dating
1991	▼ **"Frozen Man" discovered in Alps!**

eggs in its eyes. Microscopic organisms finish off what the bigger animals started. The weather, wind, and rain scatter what's left.

The Iceman avoided disappearing by chance. He died at the bottom of a gap between two large rock formations in the mountains. This shelter probably hid him from most large scavengers, such as vultures. By luck, it probably began to snow right as he died. Soon he was

The deep, narrow gap between the rocky ridges in the mountain where the Iceman lay allowed the body to escape being crushed by the glacier. *Copyright Gerhard Hinterleitner / Gamma Liaison*

covered in a white blanket. This further helped hide his body from the animals that would make a meal of it.

Somehow, and scientists are still not exactly sure how, his body was mummified. Many archaeologists believe a steadily blowing wind passed through the loosely packed snow, carrying away the moisture from his body. "He was freeze-dried," said Konrad Spindler. The Iceman was too dry to develop adipocere, or grave wax. Drying is one way to prevent decay. Egyptians mummified their pharoahs' bodies to make sure they would survive into the afterlife. More commonly, everyone from Native Americans to European explorers has dried meats and fish over smoky fires to preserve the food for long periods.

Another method to preserve meat, or a human body, is refrigeration. Extreme cold prevents decay. Think of a refrigerator.

But how did the Iceman survive the forces of the glacier? At times the ice towered 100 to 200 feet above his body, the height of a 20-story building. How was he not crushed? And why wasn't he dragged down over the mountain with the movement of the glacier? How did he remain in one piece?

Luck. The Iceman died in a deep, narrow gap between two rocky ridges. These ridges acted like train tracks.

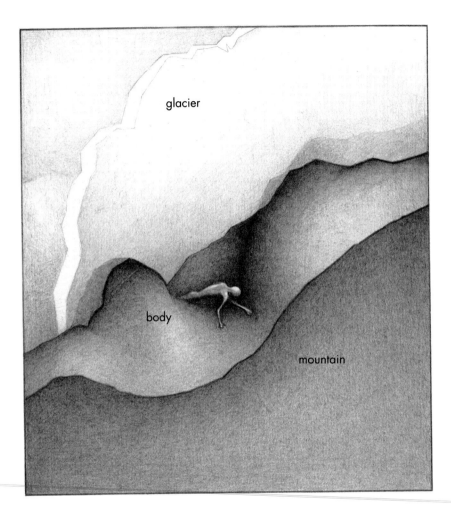

glacier

body

mountain

This cross section of the mountain shows how the glacier moved over the body on the "train tracks" of two rocky ridges.

The glacier slid down the mountain over these tracks while the Iceman lay safely beneath them.

And last, why did the Iceman suddenly appear?

In 1991 a dust storm in the Sahara Desert sent huge amounts of dust into the atmosphere. Some of this dust traveled over the Alps, where it fell and darkened the snow. Dark colors absorb more heat than light colors. This dust, along with an unusually warm summer, caused the snow to melt rapidly, exposing the Iceman for the first time in over 5,000 years!

THE BODY TALKS

3

The Iceman arrived at the University of Innsbruck in 1991 with pretty much the same body he carried around with him as he hiked the Alps thousands of years ago.

What can scientists learn from a body?

In the early 1980s archaeologists discovered the bodies of two Eskimo women who had been buried in snow for over 500 years. With the permission of the local community, researchers examined the women and found a striking connection between their health and their way of living. An autopsy on each woman showed signs of "black lung disease." This was caused from breathing in the smoke and fumes from the oil lamps they used during the long, dark Alaskan winters. The Eskimo women's arteries were clogged with fat

26

and cholesterol. This came from their diet of seal and whale. The older woman's muscles showed signs of trichinosis. This is a painful infection that may have been caused by eating uncooked polar bear meat. Clearly their bodies told stories of what it was like to be an Eskimo.

In 1957 archaeologists in Iran discovered the skeletons of seven Neanderthals who had died about 46,000 years ago. Studying just bones, archaeologists learned that one Neanderthal who had died in his late forties (quite old for a Neanderthal) had been born too crippled to take care of himself. If he couldn't take care of himself, how did he live to be an old man? Scientists could only conclude that the other Neanderthals must have taken care of him. With just bones to analyze, archaeologists learned that Neanderthals must have been caring people. Interestingly, scientists also learned from the skeleton of the crippled man that his useless arm had been amputated at the elbow. The bones spoke of surgery conducted over 46,000 years ago!

In 1984 the body of a man was found in a peat bog in Cheshire, England. This man probably died 2,000 years ago. His body was very well preserved. Studying him, researchers were able to learn what killed him, his age, his build, what he had looked like alive, his health, what he ate for his last meal, and even how it was cooked!

What will scientists learn from the man in ice?

"It's almost as if he were still alive and walked into the doctor's office," said David Fryer, an archaeologist from Kansas University. "What scientists are going to do is give this prehistoric guy a physical. And when they're done, they'll know more about him than we know about anybody else that old or older."

But how do you give a checkup to a man who has been frozen for over 53 centuries?

First, you keep him frozen. The glacier did a very good job of preserving the Iceman's body. Scientists at the University of Innsbruck realized that they needed to imitate the workings of the glacier.

Today the Iceman rests under a blanket of surgical gauze. Crushed ice made from sterilized water covers this gauze. A sterile plastic sheet covers this ice. Another layer of ice lies on top of this sheet. Blanketing this second heaping of ice is another plastic sheet. The entire package is kept inside a refrigerated room that maintains a constant humidity of 98 percent (very moist air) and a temperature of 22 degrees Fahrenheit. This humidity and temperature are identical to the conditions the Iceman experienced in his glacier. Except that this room is monitored. If the temperature were to rise just a few degrees, alarms would go off that are nearly loud enough to wake the Iceman from his long sleep. This artificial glacier is also quite expensive. Spindler estimates that it costs about $10,000 a month to maintain and study the body.

Scientists can examine the body out of the refrigerater only during the driest days of the month. Warm, moist air would cause the body to decompose. To avoid spreading germs to the body, researchers dress like surgeons, use sterilized equipment, and do their work in an environment similiar to an operating room. And then they have only 30 minutes.

Still, every time the body is removed, it begins to melt. It takes two days for it to properly refreeze. Repeated melting and freezing tear at the Iceman's cells. The more scientists study the Iceman, the more they damage him.

The rule for the researchers is to get as much information as quickly as possible, then put him back the way he was found.

The "physical" began like any checkup, with a recording of the patient's height, weight, and age.

How tall was the Iceman? Holding a tape measure to

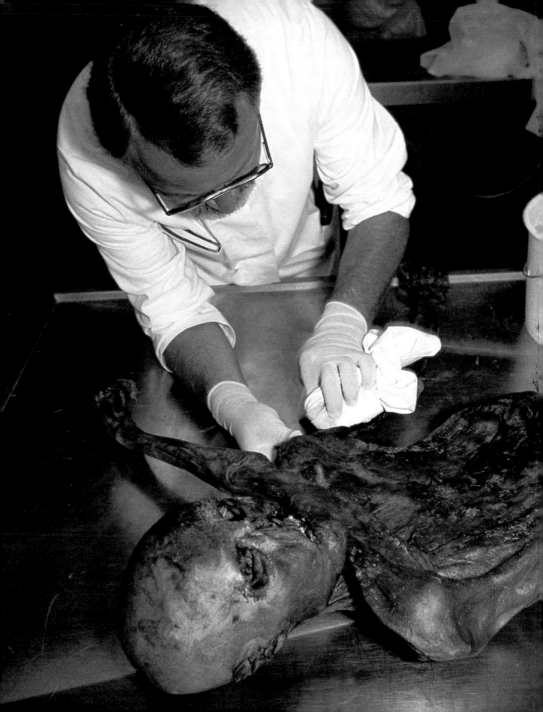

various parts of his body and taking into account that the Iceman shrank a bit as he dried out, researchers estimate his height between five feet, two inches, and five feet, four inches. To get another estimate, they measured the Iceman's femur, or thighbone. The femur is roughly one third the length of an adult's body. The exact fraction depends on where that person was born. Using special charts, archaeologists know how many times to multiply the length of a femur to get a body's height. The Iceman's femur confirmed the original estimate.

Right now the Iceman weighs about 29 pounds. This is his mummified weight. The Iceman has lost all the water from his body. Water accounts for roughly 70 percent of a person's weight while alive. Konrad Spindler estimates that the Iceman weighed about 110 pounds when he lived.

How old was the Iceman when he died? Researchers turned to his teeth. Each year of chewing and grinding wears away teeth a little more. Researchers could get an idea of the Iceman's age by examining his teeth to see how worn down they were.

A scientist examines the well-preserved Iceman. *Copyright Gerhard Hinterleitner / Gamma Liaison*

The Iceman's teeth were worn down like those of an old man. This may have been caused by the Iceman using his teeth as a tool, perhaps to soften animal skins or to cut objects. Or it may have been caused by chewing sand. Sand? At the time the Iceman lived, ancient people mixed sand into their wheat to help them grind the grain into flour. Figuring the Iceman probably crunched a lot of sand with his wheat, archaeologists estimate he was anywhere between 25 and 40 when he died.

They looked at his skull for another clue. The bones of the skull change as a person gets older. Under X rays, the Iceman's skull seemed to belong to someone between the ages of 35 and 40.

What other stories could the body tell?

Looking closely at the Iceman's skin, researchers noticed tattoos. On his lower spine are blue parallel lines. There is a cross behind his left knee and stripes on his right ankle. Normally these marks would be hidden by clothing. They weren't simply decorative. Who was supposed to see these marks? What did they mean? Why were they made?

Scientists have found a deep groove in the Iceman's right earlobe. Perhaps he wore an earring.

What did the Iceman look like when he was alive?

John Gurche, an American anthropologist and artist, set out to discover the Iceman's face.

He used photos of the mummified head, measurements of the Iceman taken by researchers, images from X rays, and information about European men to guide his sculpting. Working with assistants, Gurche spent nearly 750 hours creating a sculpture of what the Iceman may have looked like.

The Iceman's skull gave him many clues. "For example," Gurche explained, "the way his teeth come together suggested his lower lip should stick out a bit more than you see in most modern people. He's almost got an underbite. He's got a nice prominent chin and a very wide forehead. A short upper lip. A prominent nose that humps down a little. The skull indicated all of this to me."

Gurche's sculpture is made of nine layers of plastic. Each layer is tinted various flesh tones. He and his assistants often stayed up all night placing the hairs. Each hair, and there were thousands, including beard and nose hairs, was stuck in one by one.

"He looked like a thug when I first made him," Gurche said. "But his appearance softened. I even had

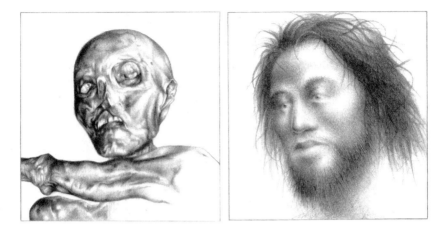

The Iceman after . . .

. . . and before. This is what he may have looked like when he was alive, according to anthropologist and artist John Gurche.

several women come into my studio and see him and say, 'Well, he's not bad looking.' I thought that was a good sign."

A male European, 35 to 40 years of age, standing five foot four and weighing around 110 pounds. Prominent chin. Short upper lip. Prominent nose that humps down a bit. Brown to blackish hair. Beard. Possible earring in right ear. Hidden tattoos. Last seen wandering the mountains at the end of the Stone Age. Missing for 5,000 years. This is who walked into the "examining room."

X rays and CAT (computerized axial tomography) scans are the tools of choice. An X ray allows researchers to get pictures of the Iceman's insides without having to cut him open. A CAT scan is a series of X rays that gives a more three-dimensional image.

Initial X rays show that the Iceman's brain has shrunk to one third its original size. His intestines have been dislocated inside his body. His left humerus (his "funny bone") reveals a fracture that may have occurred while he was alive, or in the glacier, or in the rescue.

Still, the Iceman is in pretty good shape. His body may answer hundreds of questions that scientists have about his health and nutrition.

Did he suffer from any serious childhood illnesses? What diseases did he experience? How did he take care of his teeth and gums? What was his blood type? What was his cholesterol level? What foods did he eat? What was his last meal? Will his DNA tell us who his living relatives are?

A body can talk.

The Iceman on the examining table, surrounded by the many artifacts found near his body. *Copyright Rex USA Ltd.*

THE ICEMAN GETS DRESSED 4

In the year that followed Helmut and Erika Simon's discovery, 20 feet of snow fell on the spot where the Iceman once lay. When archaeologists returned in August 1992 to look for more of the Iceman's belongings, they let the sun melt away 12 feet of that snow before they started to dig. With the help of volunteers and a machine that blew hot steam, they removed 600 tons of snow before they reached the rocky surface of the mountain. They found 400 more artifacts. These included a fur cap, the oldest of its kind ever found in Europe, part of the Iceman's bow; and a piece of the sole of one of his shoes with the stitching still in place.

The survival of the Iceman's artifacts is no less remarkable or important than the survival of his body. Artifacts made from once-living things, such as items made of leather, fur, grass, or wood, usually disintegrate quickly after they are left out in the open. Insects, mold, and microscopic organisms make a meal of these materials. The wind, rain, and snow erase what's left. Only the unusual circumstance of being buried in a room of ice beneath a glacier kept the Iceman's artifacts from disappearing. And archaeologists couldn't be happier.

Each artifact is like a piece of a jigsaw puzzle. It reveals just a little bit more about a person's life. Before the Iceman was discovered, archaeologists had very few pieces of that puzzle. Now it will be possible to see what the Iceman wore, and how he equipped himself for surviving in the treacherous Alps.

Markus Egg, an archaeologist at the Roman-Germanic Museum in Mainz, Germany, is directing this "puzzle making." He is being helped by over 120 researchers in Europe and the United States.

Egg's first job was to make sure his artifacts didn't fall apart. "Everything was wet when we got it," Egg said. "The first problem was to get that water out." Soggy artifacts rot. Drying makes them crumble, and refreezing makes them impossible to study. Every material had to be taken care of in a special way. Leather objects were carefully cleaned and dried. Industrial grease was used to replace the lost water. This preserved the leather and kept it soft enough to be handled. Wooden objects were cleaned and put into baths of warm wax. They were then removed, covered in nylon, and allowed to dry very slowly. The wax kept the wood from crumbling. Materials made from woven grass were strengthened with fluid resin, then freeze-dried.

Even after protecting these artifacts, Egg and other researchers had a difficult task ahead of them. The Iceman's clothing was terribly shredded during his "rescue." His coat arrived in Germany in hundreds of pieces. Laying these pieces out on a table, Egg and his assistants put together what they could. The shoulders are missing forever. Either the coat didn't have sleeves, or they too were lost in the recovery. Still, much can be learned. The coat is made from deer and ibex (wild goat) skin, good material for keeping somebody warm. It was sewn together with sinew (animal tendons and muscles). "I don't know who sewed his clothes," Egg said, "whether he did, or some woman in his family, but he was wearing well-sewn clothing." In addition to this fine needlework there are also places where the coat is roughly stitched together with grass threads. Archaeologists believe these were repairs made by the Iceman. Evidence that the Iceman fixed his own clothing with grass suggests that he may have been away from home a long time.

Along with his coat, archaeologists found a cape. Made from strands of skillfully woven grass, it was water repellent and probably hung over his shoulders like a poncho. Similar capes were worn by shepherds in the Alps even up to the beginning of this century.

The Iceman wore size-6 shoes. The bottom and top were made of two strips of leather sewn together, with a socklike net sewn inside. To keep his feet warm, dry, and well cushioned, the Iceman stuffed this "sock" with grasses that grew high up in the mountains. He slipped his foot inside the sock, then pulled the laces closed. Since the lacing and the sock were made of woven grass, his shoes were too delicate to take off and put on again very often. He probably wore them for long periods, repaired them constantly, and changed the grass inside only when it got too dirty or flat.

On his head the Iceman wore a half-round fur cap with a chin strap.

Did the Iceman wear pants? Long underwear? Gloves?

Artist's rendition of how the Iceman might have dressed.

No other clothing survived.

Other artifacts demonstrate the Iceman's ability to use his environment to keep himself alive. One of the stone blades found with him had traces of the 46 different types of grasses he used to construct his shoes, cape, and equipment. Next to his body were two canisters made from birch-tree bark. Inside one were maple leaves that scientists determined were picked when they were green. This indicates that the Iceman was traveling before the leaves changed color in the fall. In these leaves were a few small pieces of charcoal. Egg believes this charcoal was probably taken from one fire to be used to start another. The Iceman would not have wanted to wander the Alps without fire-making materials. Canisters like these had never been found before.

Strung together on a knotted leather cord were two mushrooms. Scientists analyzed these and found them to be *Piptoporus betulinus,* a fungus that grows on birch trees. *Piptoporus betulinus* is a natural antibiotic—it kills germs. Could these mushrooms have been part of a Stone Age first-aid kit?

In addition to using the bark and fungus from a birch tree, the Iceman boiled birch-tree roots to make gum to glue his flint arrowheads onto their shafts. These shafts were made from the wood of viburnum and dogwood trees. He also used this tree glue to stick guide feathers onto the back of his arrows. Guide feathers cause an arrow to spin as it flies, making it more accurate. Interestingly, of the 12 arrows found with the Iceman, only two were finished and ready to be fired.

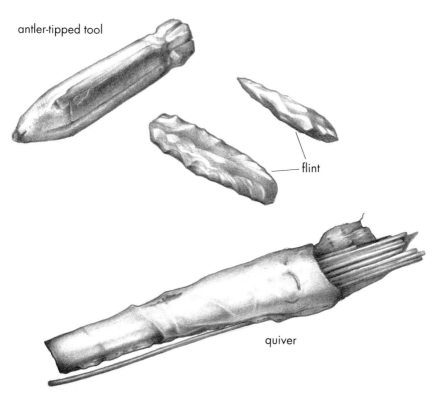

Some of the Iceman's Tools

The Iceman's bow was also unfinished. Made from the wood of a yew tree, it was five feet, 10 inches long, six inches taller than the Iceman himself. Yew is the best wood in Europe for making bows.

Christopher Bergman is an archaeologist who studies ancient weapons by building his own, then testing them. Bergman has built bows similiar to the bow found with the Iceman. These bows need some muscle to fire. To pull back their bowstrings requires the same force needed to pull back something weighing 70 to 90 pounds. "These people were not wimps," Bergman said. "We have to remember that even children were making and using these things."

Yew bows were effective weapons. "He could go after deer or ibex," Bergman explained. Most likely, the Iceman would sneak up on his prey, getting as close as possible. The bow sent stone-tip arrows shooting forth at 120 to 180 feet per second. "He could kill anything," Bergman said. "He could kill a man."

Then again, the Iceman didn't kill anything with his bow. He died before it was finished.

Yew also provided the wood for the handle of the Iceman's small ax. Archaeologists had never found a complete copper ax before, although they had found identical handles. The Iceman's ax handle is made from a naturally elbow-shaped branch. The wood is split open at one end, and the tongue-shaped blade is wedged into that split. Wet leather strips had been wrapped around the wood. When the leather dried, it shrank, making for a tight fit.

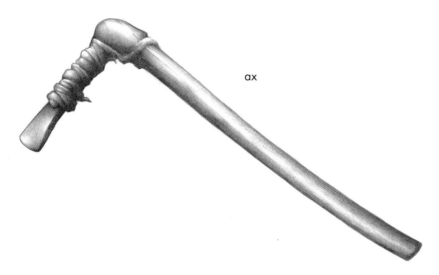

ax

Copper was the first metal used by Stone Age Europeans. Its discovery and use changed the way people lived. Before copper, people could be rich only by owning a lot of animals or a lot of wheat. It wasn't possible to travel with your riches. Copper was different. You could bring it with you, trade it, pass it on to your children.

The Iceman's blade was made by melting a chunk of rock that contained bits of copper in a pit in the earth. That furnace needed to reach at least 1,981 degrees Fahrenheit, the temperature at which copper melts. To achieve this tremendous heat, a number of people surrounded the pit, fanned the flames, and blew air through pipes onto the furnace. This fed oxygen to the fire. As the copper melted it separated from the other ingredients of the rock. Everything was then cooled. What wasn't wanted was chipped away. The copper was then remelted and poured into a cast, where it would cool and harden into the shape of a blade.

Toward the end of the Stone Age people began using copper tools as well as stone. Stone tools, such as blades, arrowheads and axes, were made by chipping away stone flakes from large pieces of rock. These flakes could be exceptionally sharp, sharper than any modern surgeon's scalpel. Copper tools, though not as sharp or strong as stone, lasted much longer. A man might go through hundreds of stone blades in a lifetime. The Iceman's ax, which he probably used as a weapon or to cut firewood, could have belonged to his family for generations. To his Stone Age contemporaries, it would have been considered something of great value.

Dagger with stone blade
and ash-wood handle

His dagger handle was from the wood of an ash tree; his arrows from viburnum trees. His backpack was made from the wood of larch and hazelwood trees; his bow and ax from yew. He wrapped his "smoldering coals" in maple leaves, which he carried in a birch-bark container. He used 46 different types of grasses for his various equipment. He carried mushrooms for medicine. His clothing was made from the skin, muscles, and tendons of deer and goat. He used the stone and copper he found in the mountains for his tools.

The Iceman dressed and equipped himself with materials from all parts of his natural world.

5

Who was the Iceman?

"We are very sure the man was a shepherd," Konrad Spindler said. "Even in our times shepherds go up to those meadows every summer for three or four months. This form of agriculture was founded in the late Stone Age and is still going strong."

The climate of the Alps was warmer in the time of the Iceman than it is today. Grass and trees grew at higher altitudes. In the spring shepherds would graze their herds lower in the valley. As the summer progressed they would drive their flocks higher up into the mountains to fresh meadows. Bears and wolves

The Iceman was probably a shepherd who grazed his herds in the mountains.

roamed the mountains, so the shepherds needed to stay with their flocks to protect them. Their days would be warm; their nights could be dangerously cold. They would leave their homes in June and then return when the first snows covered the ground in early September.

What is the evidence the Iceman was a shepherd?

He was found near a pass in the mountains that shepherds still use to herd their sheep. He wore a grass cape that was worn by shepherds into the beginning of this century. He was dressed and equipped for a long stay away from home. His restitched coat suggests that he had been on his own for some time. His shoes were well suited for mountain hiking. He had the mushrooms, which could be used as medicine if he came down with an infection. Found along with his belongings was a leather pouch, similar to a present-day "fanny pack." Inside were tools the Iceman could have used to repair his arrows, suggesting he was planning on being away from home for a while. He had begun to make a bow with his copper ax. Since it was unlikely that he would venture up into the dangerous mountains unarmed, this bow was probably a replacement for one he had lost or broken. He would need the bow to protect his animals and hunt for his own food. And then there was the ax. Copper was a rare and valued material. Only the most highly respected members of a village would own a copper ax. What could bring the Iceman such respect? Since animals were another form of wealth, guarding a flock would have made the Iceman respectable enough to own a copper ax.

Certainly, these are just clues.

"Perhaps he was a shepherd," Markus Egg said. "There are good meadows up there. But we aren't sure. We can only say perhaps."

So what went wrong?

Sometime in late August or September he died. One key piece of evidence pointing to his time of death is a small berry found with his belongings. Scientists examined this fruit under a microscope and determined it was a type of plum called a sloe berry, which ripens in late August to early September. The Iceman had probably picked it as a snack as he walked. The absence of insect eggs in his eyes also suggests he died just before the first snows.

He died lying on his left side. Archaeologists know this because the Iceman's left ear was neatly folded over. This would only have been possible had he lain on his left side, with his head raised and resting on something like a rock for a pillow.

He died without a struggle. His body shows no signs of cuts or bruises. X rays show no abnormally broken bones or damaged organs. There doesn't seem to be any medical evidence to suggest he had hurt himself and was stuck high up on the mountain. The hole in the back of his head may have been caused by a bird after he died.

He didn't die from hunger. A piece of wild-goat meat, along with some berries, was found beside him.

He wasn't frantic. The position in which the artifacts were found suggests the Iceman set them down neatly before he lay down.

He wasn't cold. Somebody who was freezing would curl up, hugging his body for warmth. The Iceman stretched out. Scientists studying the body believe he died lying on his left side, with his arms straightened down along his body. His legs were slightly spread open.

What killed the Iceman?

The Iceman in his last hours.

"We believe he went climbing around in the mountains," Konrad Spindler said. Perhaps he had gone searching for a new bow. He certainly didn't want to spend time without one. How would he hunt or protect his flock? Since he was well above where trees grew, he would have needed to climb down the mountain to find a yew tree. After cutting off a branch or cutting a sapling, he began working on the tips of the bow with his ax. At some point he started to make his way back up. Exhausted from climbing, short of breath, he may have seen a storm coming and looked for shelter. He found the gap between the two rocky ridges. Climbing down into his shelter, he spread out his gear. He might have started a fire. But being so far above where the trees grew, there couldn't have been much wood for fuel. He lay down. He was so tired, he didn't even feel discomfort from his left ear being folded over.

Within hours he was dead. The cold had killed him.

"It's not unusual," Konrad Spindler said. "Near Mont Blanc, eight climbers died yesterday."

Somehow his body dried out. Snows fell. Eventually he was trapped in a cellar of ice. Above him glaciers 200 feet tall moved relentlessly down the mountain.

For 5,000 years the Alps hid him. His fellow Europeans moved on from stone and copper tools to plastics, atomic weapons, and superconductors. They engaged in innumerable wars. They explored the mountains, other continents, the bottom of the ocean, other planets.

Scientists plan on studying the Iceman for many years. What will the Iceman continue to teach us about our past? If he could speak, what would he say about our present?

GLOSSARY AND PRONUNCIATION GUIDE

Adipocere (AD-uh-puh-seeyr): A whitish creamy or waxy substance that forms from the soft parts of a body that has been kept in a place where there is no oxygen (for example, a body stuck in a glacier lacks oxygen).

Alloy (AH-loi): A mixture of two or more metals.

Alloying (Ah-loi-ing): Blending one metal with another, usually by heating them until they become liquid. The oldest alloy is bronze, which is made by blending tin with copper. Bronze is much harder than either tin or copper and can be readily made into weapons, tools, or even decorative objects, such as statues or jewelry.

Anthropologist (an-thruh-PAH-luh-jist): A scientist who studies the history, science, or culture of people.

Antibiotic (an-tih-bye-AH-tik): A substance that can be used to destroy bacteria that cause illness. Penicillin is an antibiotic produced by a mold.

Archaeologist (are-kee-AH-luh-jist): A scientist who studies how ancient people lived.

Artifact (ARE-tih-fact): Any object made by a person. If artifacts are made out of hard materials, such as stone or metal,
they may often survive thousands of years.

Atom (AH-tum): The smallest particle of any substance.
Atoms are so small, about six million of them could fit
within the period at the end of this sentence.

Atomic (Ah-TAH-mik): Relating to atoms; using the energy
from atoms. The atom bomb and hydrogen bomb are two
atomic weapons capable of destroying entire cities.

Autopsy (AW-top-see): The examination of a dead body, often
to determine the cause of death.

CAT (computerized axial tomography) (kom-PYOU-tuh-rized
ACK-see-ulh tow-MAH-gruh-fee) *scan:* Three-dimensional
images created by a computer from a series of X rays.

Carbon dioxide (KAR-bun dye-ACK-side): A colorless gas that
is absorbed from the air by plants. Plants take in carbon
dioxide and give off oxygen. Animals, including humans,
take in oxygen and give off carbon dioxide.

Carbon 14: A rare form of carbon that is radioactive. All
plants and animals take in carbon while they are alive. A
very small fraction of that carbon is carbon 14. When a
living thing dies, its carbon 14 decays, disappearing at a
precise rate. The amount is halved every 5,730 years. If
something dies with 16 carbon-14 atoms, after 5,730 years it
will have eight. After another 5,730 years it will have four.
After another 5,730 only two carbon-14 atoms will remain.
After 22,920 years, or four halvings, there will be one car-
bon-14 atom.

Carbon-14 dating, or radiocarbon dating: Determining how much carbon-14 decay has taken place to estimate when something lived. For example, if there were eight carbon-14 atoms in a bone to begin with and now there are two, that sample has halved twice, or gone through approximately 11,460 years of decay.

Carbon 12: The common form of carbon. There are a trillion (a million million) regular carbon atoms in the atmosphere for every atom of carbon 14.

Cholesterol (Kuh-LESS-tuh-rol): Soapy, waxy substance produced by the digestion of fats that may contribute to heart disease.

Decay (dih-KAY): To decrease gradually or rot.

DNA (Deoxyribonucleic acid) (dee-ACK-sih-rye-bow-noo-klay-ick AH-sid): A molecule that contains the coded directions for how a cell will develop and function. DNA determines such things as hair and eye color.

Dogwood: A tree with heads of small flowers.

Femur (FEE-mur): The thighbone.

Finail (Fin-EYEL) *Peak:* The second-highest mountain peak in the Ötztal Alps.

Flint: A hard stone used by prehistoric people for tools and weapons. Flint can be chipped, creating flakes that are as sharp as surgical tools.

Forensic (fuh-REN-sick) *medicine:* A science that uses medical information to answer questions relating to the law. A forensic scientist might study a damaged bone to learn what weapon was used to create that wound.

Fungus: A group of living things that includes molds, mushrooms, and mildews.

Glacier (GLAY-shur): A flowing river of ice that can be hundreds of feet thick. Glaciers form on mountains as more and more snow falls. The snow on the ground becomes compacted and turns to ice.

Humerus (HYOO-muh-rus): The long bone of the upper arm, sometimes called the funny bone.
Hypothesis (hi-PAH-thuh-sus): An idea that is based on careful thought but that has not been scientifically tested.

Ibex (EYE-becks): A wild goat that lives high in the mountains and has long, curved horns.
Innumerable (ih-NOOM-ruh-bull): Too many to count.

Metallurgist (MEH-tehl-ur-jist): Someone working with the science of metals.
Microscopic (my-kruh-SKAH-pick): Too small to be seen without the use of a microscope.
Mummify (MUH-mih-fye): To dry out a dead body so that even its soft parts, such as its skin, hair, and facial features, will last thousands of years.

Neanderthal (Nee-AN-dur-tall): Living approximately 100,000 years ago to 35,000 years ago, Neanderthals were closely related to modern humans. They used tools of bone, antler, and flint; wore clothes to protect themselves from the cold; created art; buried their dead; and took care of their infirm.

Organism (OR-guh-nih-zum): A living thing, such as a plant, an animal, or a bacterium.
Ötztal Alps (OHTZ-tahl): Mountains situated between Austria and Italy.

Piptoporus betulinus (pip-toe-POH-rus beh-too-LEE-nus): A wood fungus, found on birch trees, that has been known to have antibiotic effects for over 2,000 years.
Prehistory (PRE-his-tuh-ree): The study of people who lived before the invention of writing.
Prominent (Prah-muh-nunt): Pushing forward.
Protohistory (PROE-too-his-tuh-ree): The study of people who lived near the beginning of written history.

Radiocarbon dating. See Carbon-14 dating.

Scrotum (SKROH-tum): The pouch in males that contains the testes.
Shaft: The body of an arrow.
Similaun Glacier (SIH-mih-lown GLAY-shur): The glacier in which the Iceman was found.
Sinew (SIN-you): Tendons and muscles used for making bowstrings and for sewing.
Superconductor (soo-puhr-kon-DUK-tur): A material that conducts electricity without turning any of that electrical energy into heat energy.

Technology (teck-NAH-luh-jee): The use of scientific knowledge to make and use tools.

Tendon (TEN-dun): The strong white fibrous tissues that connect muscles to bones.

Tomography (toe-MAH-gruh-fee): An X ray showing a cross section of bone.

Trichinosis (tri-kuh-NO-sus): A disease marked by muscular pain, high fever, and swelling, caused by eating undercooked meat infested with trichina worms.

Tutankhamen (Tuh-tan-KAH-mun): A king of Egypt who ruled over 3,000 years ago. Archaeologist Howard Carter discovered King Tutankhamen's mummy in 1922. Its face was covered in a dazzling gold mask.

Viburnum (vye-BUR-num): A tree with white or pink flowers.

X rays: Images that can be made of the inside of the body. In X rays bones show up as white and soft tissues are dark.

Yew (YOO): An evergreen tree with spiky leaves.

BIBLIOGRAPHY

Ambach, W., E. Ambach, and W. Tributsch. "Austria: Tyrol's Ice-Man." *The Lancet*, Vol. 339 (1992), p. 1471.

Bahn, Paul, and Colin Renfrew. *Archaeology: Theories, Methods, and Practice.* New York: Thames and Hudson, 1991.

Fowler, Brenda. "Scientists Enthralled by Bronze Age Body," *New York Times*, 1 October 1991, pp. C1, C10.

Fritz, Sandy. "Who Was the Iceman?" *Popular Science*, Vol. 242 (1993), pp. 46–50, 88.

Harrigan, Stephen. "The Long-Lost Hunter." *Audubon*, Vol. 94 (1992), pp. 92–96.

Jaroff, Leon. "Iceman." *Time*, Vol. 140 (1992), pp. 62–69.

McIntosh, Jane. *The Practical Archaeologist.* London: Paul Press, Ltd., 1986.

Montalbano, William. "From the Ice Comes a Mystery," *Los Angeles Times*, 21 October 1991, pp. A10, A12.

New York Public Library Desk Reference. New York: Webster's New World, 1989.

Nova. Video and transcript of "Iceman," 10 November 1992.

"On Ice 4,000 Years, Bronze Age Man Is Found," *New York Times*, 26 September 1991, p. A15.

Reisenberger, Boyce. "Iceman Yields Details of Stone Age Transition," *Washington Post*, 15 October 1992, p. A1.

Roberts, David. "The Ice Man: Lone Voyager from the Copper Age." *National Geographic*, Vol. 183, No. 6 (1993), pp. 36–37.

Ross, Philip. "Eloquent Remains." *Scientific American*, Vol. 266 (1992), pp. 114–25.

Schwartz, Jeffrey. *What the Bones Tell Us.* New York: Henry Holt, 1993.

Seidler, Horst, et al. "Some Anthropological Aspects of the Prehistoric Tyrolean Ice Man." *Science*, Vol. 258 (1992), pp. 455–57.

Sjovold, Torstein. "Frost and Found." *Natural History*, Vol. 102, No. 4 (1993), pp. 60–63.

———. "The Stone Age Iceman from the Alps: The Find and the Current Status of Investigation." *Evolutionary Anthropology*, Vol. 1, No. 4 (1992), pp. 117–24.

Stein, Mark. "Iceman Studied at Glacial Pace, Critics Charge," *Los Angeles Times*, 4 March 1993, p. A14.

INDEX

(Page numbers in *italic* refer to illustrations.)

About the Author

David Getz, the author of the middle-grade novels *Thin Air* and *Almost Famous*, is an elementary-school science teacher and staff trainer in New York City.